D1489554

My Cousin Has Eight Legs!

Words and Pictures
by

JASPER TOMKINS

SASQUATCH BOOKS

Seattle

For the grand guardians at the base of Plowboy—
the tour guides who first took me to the trees,
the lakes, the rivers, the mountains,
and the great, vast sea.

One day an octopus slithered out of his cave in Puget Sound and covered the entrance with rocks and sand. When all was well hidden, he said good-bye to his home and rose slowly through the water, up toward the sparkling sunlight.

On the surface the ocean was wild and free. The octopus let the waves carry him to new places and adventures. He was taking a vacation.

The next afternoon the octopus was nearly run over by a large ferryboat full of cars and people. Instead of ducking out of the way, he slapped a long arm onto the side of the ferry and hitched a ride. When he was rested, the octopus stuck some of his legs up and pulled himself out of the water and onto the main deck. He slid under a big truck and then noticed a red station wagon with one window rolled down just a bit. It looked like the perfect place to hide!

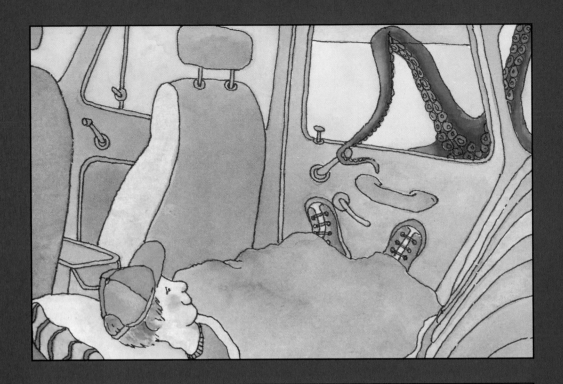

Well, I was in that car and sound asleep in the back
seat. I had gone with my dad to visit a man who lived
on an island, and I had played on the beach all day
while they talked business.

I was dreaming about being a fish when suddenly I
woke up. There was an octopus arm squeezing through
the crack at the top of the window! I didn't even think to
be afraid. The arm stretched lower and lower and then
started rolling down the window. Pretty soon, there was
a whole octopus sitting on the seat right next to me.

"What are you doing in here?" I whispered.

"My name is Victor and I like to travel," responded the octopus happily. "I'm going home with you for part of my vacation."

"But my dad will be back any minute," I protested.

The octopus laughed. "I assure you he won't even notice. You'll see, we're going to have a great time. Just pretend you're asleep again and I'll hide on the floor."

Before I lay down, I threw part of my blanket over his head, just to be safe.

When the ferry pulled in to the dock, my dad came down from the upper deck and started the car.

"Are you still there?" he asked.

"Yes," I said with a tired voice.

"Go ahead and sleep, and I'll have us home in time for dinner," he said as we drove down the ramp off the ferry.

I was about to tell him about the octopus when someone called him on his car phone. He talked the rest of the way home.

My new friend raised up two arms and shaped them to look like little heads acting out the phone conversation. Then he moved his arms up higher and made them look like big ears on the sides of my dad's head. I had to duck under the blanket to keep from laughing out loud.

Victor and I had a great time in the back seat. I tied his legs together in knots, but he always figured out a way to undo himself. He took one of my shoes and passed it from one suction cup to another, all the way down one of his legs, without dropping it. Then we played checkers until the car bumped up the driveway at home.

Dad opened the front door, and I pointed to my bedroom window while Victor watched from the car. Then I went inside to say hi to my mom. After dinner I said I was going to bed early and hurried to my room.

I was surprised to see that Victor had already let himself in. Not only that, he was taking a bath in my very own bathtub. What a time he was having! Each of his eight arms and legs was doing something different. I didn't know a bath could be so much fun. I jumped in with my little red boat and took it on a cruise through the tropical islands and wild storms that Victor made.

After our bath we wrapped ourselves in big towels and sat in front of the heater. We were both too tired to stay awake, so I said good night and told my new friend I was glad he had found me. I got into bed, and Victor crawled back into the bathtub. He said he wanted to be close to the water.

In the morning, I didn't want to go to school. I wanted to stay home and play with Victor. I went into the bathroom and there he was, standing in front of the mirror with some of my clothes on.

"What are you doing?" I asked.

"I'm going to school with you," he said. "I'm your new cousin."

He really did look just like any other kid, except that he had no hands. I gave him a pair of my mittens, and he folded up the tips of two arms inside them.

He showed me the note he'd written to my teacher. It looked just like my dad's handwriting. The note explained that my cousin would be visiting for the day.

I laughed all the way to the bus stop as Victor learned how to walk. He was very awkward at first, but by the time I introduced him to my friends, he was doing fine.

When we got to class, Mrs. Foster was a little upset about having to find a desk for my cousin, but she couldn't help liking Victor. He opened the door for her, and during morning recess, he cleaned all the blackboards. Of course, only I knew how he did it so fast.

After lunch my cousin was the star of the playground. No one could beat him at tetherball or at shooting baskets. Then he showed us amazing tricks on the hanging rings.

Back in class my cousin got a 100 on the geography test, and in science he explained how ocean tides work. Even Mrs. Foster was fascinated. When we went into the computer lab, Victor started pushing buttons and made things appear on his screen that no one had ever seen before.

At the end of the day, everyone said good-bye to my cousin, and Mrs. Foster invited him to visit again anytime.

Victor and I had a snack when we got home, but he didn't want to watch TV. He said he didn't feel good when it was on. So we went out to climb trees. He was the first friend I'd ever had who could figure out the secret way to my tree house. We stayed up there for a long time watching the changing clouds over Mount Rainier. Then, back on the ground, we played hide-and-seek. But I could never find Victor. He squeezed into small places I would never think of looking.

When my mom called me in to eat, Victor sneaked through my bedroom window. I ate dinner and talked with my parents until they left for a meeting in town.

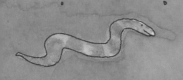

I sat with Victor on the floor of my room. He described what it felt like to be an octopus, and he told me to pretend we were together in the sea. I closed my eyes and I was there. We went to secret caves that had doorways so small I didn't see how we could possibly get in. But Victor taught me to relax my body and flow right through the openings, just like water. We ate crabs, and clams and other things I usually don't like, but they were all yummy when I was an octopus.

My favorite thing we did together was to slowly rise up toward the waves and then gently drift back down to the bottom of the sea. I felt like I was in outer space.

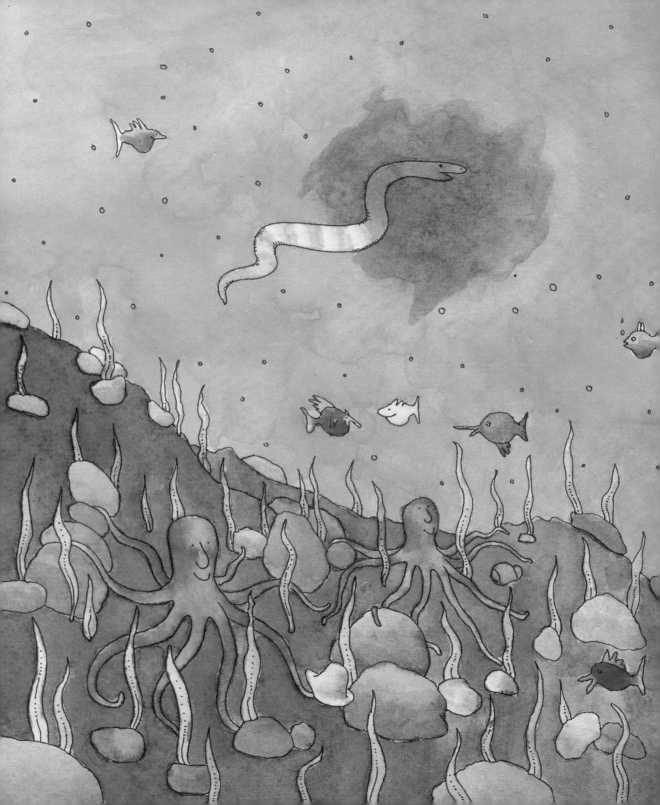

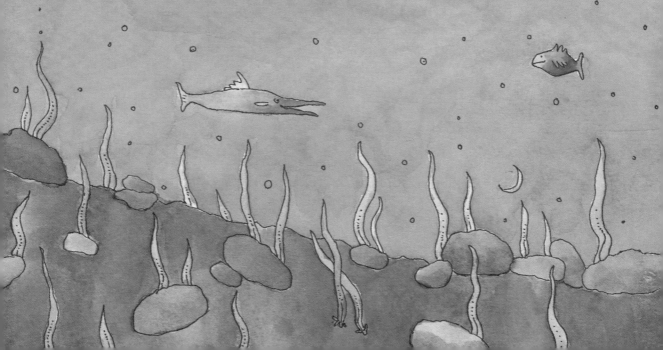

A big eel chased us, but my cousin told me what to do. I squirted some special octopus ink and darted away. Victor and I quickly changed color and made our skins lumpy, so we looked like the rocks and seaweed. After the eel came out of the cloud of black ink, he couldn't find us, and so he finally went on his way.

When my cousin said it was time to go back, I had almost forgotten I wasn't really an octopus. I opened my eyes and gave Victor a big hug as he slid into the bathtub. And then I hopped right into bed.

When I got up the next morning, Victor had already left. There was only a note saying he'd be back after dark. All day I wondered where he could have gone. I was reading in my room that evening when he finally pushed the window open. He looked very cold.

"Where have you been?" I whispered. But he didn't say a word until he was in a hot bath with lots of salt. He had gone to Mount Rainier. I couldn't believe it!

"I must have been close to the top," he said, "but I fell into a crevasse. And even though I have 1,920 suction cups on my arms and legs, they just don't work on ice. If only I had some hiking boots."

A mountain goat had helped him find a way out of danger. And, as if that wasn't enough, Victor admitted he had taken the car to the mountain after seeing my dad leave for work on the bus.

"How did you know how to drive?" I asked. Victor said it was easy after watching what my dad did on the way home from the ferry. He promised he would somehow pay for the gas he had used.

The next morning, Victor left a note saying he was going to get a job. He can't be serious! I thought to myself.

That night my cousin was waiting in my room. He was holding some money and couldn't wait to tell me about his jobs. In the morning he had picked apples at an orchard over the hill, and the farmers said he was the fastest picker ever. In the afternoon he swept the floors of a construction site. It was supposed to take four hours, but he was done in half an hour. He made enough money to pay for the gas, but he said he still needed some more to buy a special surprise. I could tell Victor was quite proud of himself.

"This is the best vacation I've ever had," he said.

The following night Victor told me about his day stocking shelves at a supermarket. The managers liked his work so much that they gave him a big case of potato chips.

"Watch this," he said, and opened up three of the bags. He took out the chips and passed them one by one up his arms from sticker to sticker. Soon he had five arms completely covered. He stood up on three legs and made the chips flutter like they were in the wind, and some of them sailed to the floor. He changed colors and looked like a great tree in a fall wind, with leaves piling up around the trunk. I loved my cousin.

The next afternoon at school when the final bell rang, I was the first one out the door. I was surprised to see my dad waving to me from the parking lot. I hopped into the car and we drove off immediately. And then I started laughing because it wasn't my dad at all. It was Victor! He was dressed in some of my dad's clothes.

Victor had hidden in the back of the car when my dad drove to work. Once the car was parked and my dad was up in his office, Victor set off for more adventures before coming to pick me up. He even visited the Woodland Park Zoo.

We left the car in my dad's parking space at work and walked the two blocks to the waterfront. I was excited to be downtown with my cousin.

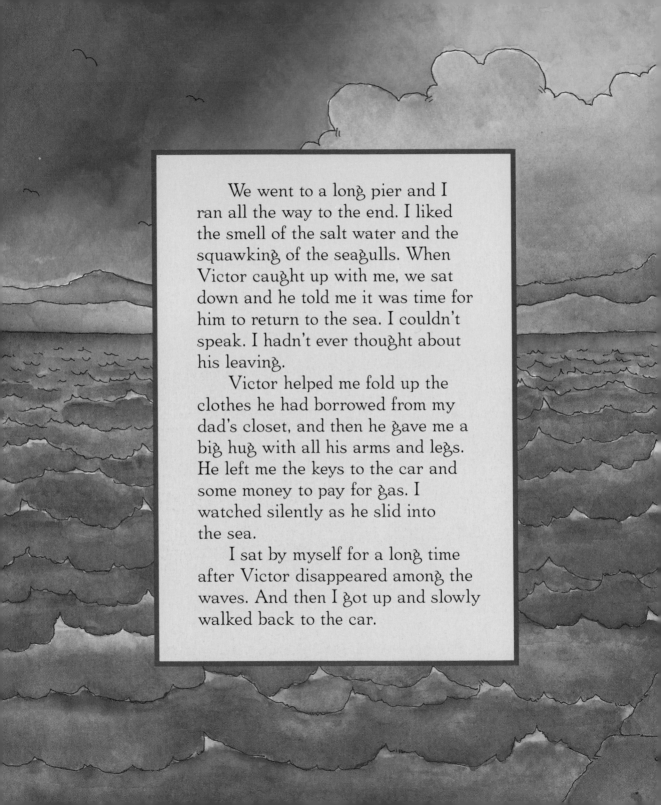

We went to a long pier and I ran all the way to the end. I liked the smell of the salt water and the squawking of the seagulls. When Victor caught up with me, we sat down and he told me it was time for him to return to the sea. I couldn't speak. I hadn't ever thought about his leaving.

Victor helped me fold up the clothes he had borrowed from my dad's closet, and then he gave me a big hug with all his arms and legs. He left me the keys to the car and some money to pay for gas. I watched silently as he slid into the sea.

I sat by myself for a long time after Victor disappeared among the waves. And then I got up and slowly walked back to the car.

I could have gone to my dad's office to wait for him,
but I didn't think I'd be able to talk yet. So I decided to
wait in the back seat. I opened the door and there was
a big package waiting for me from my cousin. I tore it
open and I cried. But I was happy, too, because I knew
that somehow I would see Victor again.

I put on my new flippers and mask and lay down to
think about my wonderful friend. By the time my dad
found me, I was sound asleep.

ABOUT THE OCTOPUS

An octopus is truly a remarkable creature. It is aware of everything that goes on in its environment. It is very smart and very clever. An octopus moves with great agility and surprising speed. It is also quite cautious and secretive. A master of camouflage, it hides by changing the color and texture of its skin to match nearby surroundings. When attacked, an octopus releases a cloud of dark ink, which both confuses the attacker and numbs its senses. If captured, an octopus can remember how the latches were fastened on the cage and let itself out when no one is looking.

An octopus has eight arms (or legs), which are lined with two rows of powerful suction cups. These cups are so well controlled that an octopus can pass a piece of food along an arm from one suction cup to the next, right into its mouth. An octopus can even open up jars by twisting off the tops. It usually eats crabs and other marine life, often leaving shells piled outside the entrance to the cave it lives in.

A female octopus lays about 200,000 eggs. When the eggs hatch, the baby octopuses are barely larger than the head of a pin, yet they must fend for themselves because their mother dies within days of their birth. Unfortunately, most of the young will be eaten by other sea creatures and only one or two will survive into adulthood. Eventually, an octopus can grow as large as twenty to thirty feet in diameter.

Some of the world's largest octopuses live in the waters of Puget Sound near Seattle, Washington. In that home and other saltwater homes worldwide, octopuses must deal with increasing pollution and other environmental disruptions as they struggle to continue living in their quiet ways.

ABOUT THE AUTHOR

Jasper Tomkins lives near Mount Rainier in Washington
State. He is the author and illustrator of *The Catalog,
Nimby, The Hole in the Ocean, Bear Sleep Soup,*
and other stories for children. He had his first
encounter with an octopus when he was on a
fishing boat in Puget Sound.

Copyright ©1992 by Jasper Tomkins
Third printing 1997

Printed in Hong Kong.

Library of Congress Cataloging-in-Publication Data

Tomkins, Jasper.
My cousin has eight legs!/words and pictures by Jasper Tomkins
p.   cm
Summary: Follows the adventures of a young boy
and an octopus who poses as his cousin.

ISBN 0-912365-68-4 : $9.95

[1. Octopus—Fiction.] I. Title.
PZ7. T586Mx   1992   92-21940
[E]—dc20

Sasquatch Books
615 Second Avenue
Seattle, Washington 98104
(206)467-4300
books@sasquatchbooks.com
http://www.sasquatchbooks.com